CHINA

PHILIP STEELE

A⁺

Smart Apple Media

EMERGING
NATIONS

CHINA

A⁺

Smart Apple Media

Published by Smart Apple Media, an imprint of Black Rabbit Books
P.O. Box 3263, Mankato, Minnesota 56002
www.blackrabbitbooks.com

Published by arrangement with the Watts Publishing Group LTD, London.

Cataloging-in-Publication Data is available from the Library of Congress
ISBN 978-1-59920-987-6 (library binding)
ISBN 978-1-62588-601-9 (eBook)

Series Editor: Julia Bird
Series Advisor: Emma Epsley, geography teacher and consultant
Series Design: sprout.uk.com

Photo credits:

Mira Agrou/Dreamstime: 39br. Andersen/Dreamstime: 15tl. Andrey Bayda/Shutterstock: 40. Natalie Behring/Aurora Photos/Alamy: 16. Bjshanshan/Dreamstime: front cover t. Chameleonseye/Shutterstock: 20b. Hung Chung Chih/Shutterstock: 14t, 18. Chungking/Shutterstock: 6. Pierro Crucuatti/Shutterstock: 19, 33. EPA/Alamy: 12. Eprom/Dreamstime: 11. 5dmarkii/Dreamstime: 38b. Gary718/Shutterstock: 9. Svilen Georgiev/Shutterstock: 21t. Hannamariah/Shutterstock: 31t. Robert Harding PL: 39t. Imagine China: 17, 27. Imagine China/Corbis: 28. Interfoto/Alamy: 8. Jianbinglee/Dreamstime: 31b. Keystone USA-ZUMA/Rex Features: 42. Kingqil/Dreamstime: 13. Lidacheng/Dreamstime: 25t. Liumantiger/Dreamstime: 26. Mamahoohooba/Shutterstock: 23. Meanmachine77/istockphoto: 15bl. Paop/Dreamstime: 22. Xiao Peichen/Dreamstime: 43. Jack Q/Shutterstock: 34. Cora Reed/Shutterstock: 37. Reuters/Corbis: 41. Sergei/Dreamstime: 35b. Lee Snider/Dreamstime: 39bl. Spirit of America/Shutterstock: 20t. Keren Su/Corbis: 25b. Alvin Teo/Dreamstime: 36. Testing/Shutterstock: 10. TonyV3112/Shutterstock: 15tr, 21b, 30, 32, 38t. Guo Yu/Shutterstock: 14b. Liu Yu/Corbis: 35t. Yu-he Zhang/Dreamstime: 24. Xi Zhang/Dreamstime: front cover bLiang Zhao/Dreamstime: 15br.

Printed in the United States by CG Book Printers
North Mankato, Minnesota

PO 1721
3-2015

987654321

CHINA

CONTENTS

INTRODUCING CHINA

The Oriental Pearl TV Tower soars 1,535 feet (468 m) above Shanghai's Pudong district. Before the 1990s, this was an undeveloped area of docks and fields.

CHINA AND CHANGE

Skyscrapers of glass and steel soar on the Beijing skyline. Tall cranes tower above building sites. Poor country people crowd into railway stations and travel in search of a new life in the growing cities.

China is changing more quickly than any other nation. After centuries of hardship, this vast country now has the world's second largest economy after the United States. Can this rise to riches be sustained? It is too early to say, but this is certainly a dynamic, exciting time to live in China.

NEW DIRECTIONS

These changes do not just affect the world of work or politics but transform every aspect of people's lives in China. Changes have a huge impact upon the environment, health, family life, even people's eating habits and pastimes. Can China's ancient traditions and customs survive in this age of new technologies, social media, and the Internet? The big shifts in China impact all of us around the world. You may find Chinese-made toys, clothes, or computers in your own home, or a Chinese company may own your local factory. China has gone global.

RUSSIA

KAZAKHSTAN

MONGOLIA

ALTAI MTS

TIAN SHAN MTS

Urumqi

KYRGYZSTAN

XINJIANG UYGHUR

TAJIKISTAN

TAKLAMAKAN DESERT

GHANISTAN

Harbin

Beijing

NORTH KOREA

Tianjin

SOUTH KOREA

Yellow Sea

JAPAN

CHINA

Huang He (Yellow River)

Da Yunhe (Grand Canal)

PAKISTAN

TIBET

Xian

East China Sea

Chengdu

Suzhou

Shanghai

HONG KONG

HIMALAYA MOUNTAINS

Lhasa

Chongqing

Wuhan

NEPAL

EVEREST

BHUTAN

Chang Jiang (Yangtse)

Hangzhou

BANGLADESH

Fuzhou

Guangzhou

TAIWAN

INDIA

BURMA
(MYANMAR)

VIETNAM

Zhu Jiang (Pearl River)

Xiamen

Shenzhen

LAOS

HAINAN

South China Sea

THAILAND

PHILIPPINES

MACAU

SRI LANKA

SPOTLIGHT ON CHINA

CHINA FULL NAME: People's Republic of China • AREA: 3.7 million square miles (9.6 million km²) • POPULATION: 1.362 billion • Capital: Beijing (21 million) • BIGGEST CITY: Shanghai (24 million) • SPECIAL ADMINISTRATIVE REGIONS: Hong Kong, Macau • LONGEST RIVER: Chang Jiang/Yangtze 3,900 miles (6,300 km) • HIGHEST MOUNTAIN: Qomolangma/Everest 5.5 miles (8,850 m) • NATURAL RESOURCES: Coal, iron ore, oil, natural gas, tin, tungsten, uranium

A TRIP TO CHINA

The People's Republic of China is big and beautiful. It takes up nearly 3.7 million square miles (9.6 million km²) of eastern Asia. It has bitterly cold winters in the north, but a warm and humid **subtropical** climate in the south. Floods, earthquakes, and **typhoons** are common.

Western China is bordered by some of the world's highest mountain ranges, including the Himalayas. It also has remote, harsh deserts such as the Taklamakan and the wide open grassy steppes of Inner Mongolia.

In the eastern half of China, two long, broad rivers, the Huang He (Yellow River) and the Chang Jiang (Yangtze), flow eastward across great plains to the sea. The soil has been farmed and built upon for thousands of years. Most Chinese people still live on these plains and coasts. China has the largest population on the planet and is home to over 1.36 billion people. One-fifth of the world's population are citizens of China.

PEOPLE & NATION
A LONG HISTORY

Qin Shi Huangdi was the first emperor of a united China. He died in 210 BC.

PAST TO PRESENT

The rapid changes taking place in China today are not happening in a new country. The changes are rooted in one of the oldest civilizations on Earth. China has a long history of innovation. Chinese inventors gave the world paper, gunpowder, printing, and compasses.

AN ANCIENT EMPIRE

China became a single empire in 221 BC and remained under the strict rule of emperors until the 1900s. China was often isolated and locked in tradition. At other times, it engaged with the rest of the world. For many centuries, goods such as tea and silk were traded overland to western Asia and Europe.

By the 1700s and 1800s, China was being surpassed by the new industrial nations of Europe. Weak emperors gave away control of key Chinese cities and ports to foreigners. In 1912, the last emperor, Puyi, was overthrown and China became a republic.

YEARS OF TURMOIL

Troubled years lay ahead. Warlords, leaders with private armies, seized control in some regions. Communists, seeking to give power to poor peasants and workers, battled with the Nationalists. In the 1930s, neighboring Japan invaded many areas. By 1949, the Communists controlled all of China. The Nationalists fled to the island of Taiwan and formed a rival government. The new Communist state faced hostility from the United States and its allies.

THE PEOPLE'S REPUBLIC

Grounded in centuries of poverty and social injustice, the People's Republic of China faced many problems in its early years. Communist leader Mao Zedong (1893–1976) nationalized industry, so it was run by the state. He took farmland from landlords and gave it to the peasants, who had to take part in shared farming projects. The changes, known as the Great Leap Forward, were radical and often resulted in violence and great hardship. Some Communist Party members called for a change of direction. They were accused of betrayal by more radical members, who idolized Mao. In the 1960s, this led to a period of chaos and strife.

NEW ORDER

Mao died in 1976. A new leader, Deng Xiaoping, changed China's economic policy and brought in foreign investment. Relations with the West improved. This new China became very different from what Mao had envisaged. It was the start of the China we know today.

A portrait of Mao Zedong still overlooks the gateway to Beijing's Imperial Palace.

中华人民共和国万岁　世界人民大团结万岁

MEET THE PEOPLE

In the large Chinese cities, people enjoy crowding around a table to chat, argue, and joke. People in China's cities always have lived at close quarters with their neighbors and shared space. The Special Administrative Region of Macau is the most densely packed territory in the world. With 19,610 people to .4 square miles (1 km²), China is four times as crowded as London.

POPULATION PRESSURE

China's population is expected to peak at about 1.5 billion in 2033. A large population creates a large and active workforce. However, all those people need food and use precious resources, such as water. Careful planning is necessary. Censuses have been held in China for more than 2,000 years, but surveying today's vast population is a difficult task. In 2010, it took 6.5 million temporary officials to check approximately 400 million households! The census confirmed that the rate at which the population was growing had slowed down.

ONE-CHILD POLICY

Since 1979, most couples living in cities have only been allowed to have one baby. This rule may have prevented 400 million births, but it caused much unhappiness and social problems. The one-child rule has already been relaxed in Shanghai and other cities may follow.

People shop in crowded downtown Macau, a Special Administrative Region of China.

BOYS OR GIRLS?

A preference for boys is traditional in a land that relies on manual labor for income. Since the scanning of pregnancies became common, the number of abortions of girl babies has increased. Approximately 119 boys are born for every 100 girls in some regions. This is a humanitarian tragedy that could lead to a generation of Chinese men being unable to find wives in the future.

PEOPLE AND LANGUAGES

More than 9 out of 10 Chinese belong to the Han ethnic group. The rest belong to 55 smaller groups. Each has different customs, beliefs, and languages. These minorities are called nationalities. While they make up a small proportion of the total, they occupy over half of the land area. Tensions between ethnic groups are often high, especially in the far northwest and in Tibet where many people oppose Chinese rule and settlement by Han Chinese.

The main language of China is Putonghua or Standard Chinese and also is known as Mandarin. Many other variants and dialects of Chinese are spoken across China. Some very different languages, such as Mongolian, Tibetan, and Uyghur are also spoken.

A new baby faces a new China. What will the future hold?

11

WHO GOVERNS?

Before becoming Chinese leader, Xi Jinping had already visited the United States to discuss trade with President Barack Obama.

LEADING MAN

In 2012, a new Chinese leader stepped onto the red-carpeted stage at the Great Hall of the People in Beijing. Xi Jinping (pronounced SHEE jin BING) had been chosen as General Secretary of the Communist Party of China (CPC). Xi had won control of the world's biggest political party with more than 80 million members.

Big screens on the street showed Xi's speech, but most Chinese people knew little about him. But they probably knew of his wife, popular singer Peng Liyuan. Chinese politics are less public than in the West. Larger-than-life figures such as Mao are no longer welcome. Confirmed as president in March 2013, Xi Jinping has an easy public manner. Whether or not he will be a reformer remains to be seen.

HOW POLITICS WORKS

The Communist Party of China controls China's political system. Although China has eight other small parties, these are all in alliance with the CPC. No free elections are held between competing parties. Within the CPC, members often hold very different opinions. Behind the scenes, different factions jostle for power.

In, China citizens over 18 can vote every five years for Local People's Congresses. The members who are elected vote for a National People's Congress (NPC), which chooses the officials who make the laws. Women have played a much more prominent part in Chinese society since 1948, but few reach the top jobs. The key roles in the CPC are still mostly held by men.

CORRUPTION IN CHINA

As soon as Xi Jinping took power, he promised to tackle corruption. Dishonesty has been a serious problem in the Communist Party and government for many years. Bribery, illegal property schemes, and fraud are common. Government contracts are often awarded to friends or family. People with powerful connections may escape prosecution for a crime. An increase in public anger makes Xi's anti-corruption campaign a priority.

Corruption reaches to the top. Li Jianguo, vice chairman of China's parliament, was investigated for engineering his nephew's appointment to a government role.

OUTSIDE THE NPC

China has regional governments in its provinces and city-based municipalities. Autonomous regions, having a separate ethnic identity, are given greater powers to make their own laws. Hong Kong and Macau are former colonies of Britain and Portugal. They are called Special Administrative Regions and have their own political and legal systems.

CHINA AND COMMUNISM

The Chinese party system is typically communist, but China's economic policies are not. Communism aims to ensure that working people receive the full reward for the things they make or the work they do. Profits should not be paid to investors and shareholders to accumulate private wealth or capital. Capitalism was bitterly opposed under Mao Zedong, but China now welcomes private companies making profit. However, the state or regional governments still own many companies and direct the economy.

CITY OF CHANGE

Beijing may not be China's biggest city and has not always been the national capital But for much of its history, it has been a great center of political power. Decisions made in Beijing still affect the whole of this vast country, just as they did when emperors ruled China from Beijing's Imperial Palace. This complex of splendid halls and spacious courtyards, behind red walls and a moat, forms a city within the city.

On a frosty winter's day, the tiled roofs of Beijing's historical palaces and temples look glorious in the sun. You may see colorful kites soaring against a blue sky and tugged by icy winds blowing all the way from Mongolia. Chinese visitors and overseas tourists throng the city's ancient monuments or travel north of the city to visit ancient tombs or the Great Wall of China.

However, concrete high-rise buildings and expressways have now replaced most of old Beijing and filled in its tree-lined canals. The streets are filled with people hurrying to work amid chaotic traffic. As more and more city dwellers drive cars, exhaust fumes often create a hazy smog that hangs in the air. Welcome to Beijing, a city of constant change. Its municipality, the greater urban district, is home to more than 21 million people.

The old Imperial Palace is known as the Forbidden City because ordinary people were not allowed to pass inside its gates or to glimpse the emperor.

Tiantan, the beautiful Temple of Heaven, dates back to the 1400s. Emperors used to pray here for a good harvest.

Tiananmen Square is a huge area bordering the Imperial Palace and the massive Great Hall of the People. In 1989, it was at the center of political protests demanding democratic reform, but these were brutally put down.

Modern Beijing has become a city of high-rise housing, international hotels, offices, and factories.

The traditional housing for the ordinary folk of Beijing was made up of low buildings around a courtyard that bordered narrow lanes and alleys. Most of these hutongs are now gone.

The National Stadium built for the Beijing Olympics in 2008 was nicknamed the Bird's Nest! While the successful Olympic Games presented a new image of the city to the world, approximately 300,000 people lost their homes to make way for construction.

CHAPTER 2

LAND & WORK
ECONOMIC BOOM

MAKING A LIVING

More than 36 percent of China's workers farm the land while 27 percent have jobs in factories or mines. Most of the remainder find work providing services. These include nursing, teaching, or office jobs. Working long hours in a hotel may be tiring. But for many, it offers an easier life than in the farming village back home, and the work is better paid.

THE BIG BOOM

Since 1978, China's gross domestic product has increased tenfold. China is now the world's biggest exporter. Global economic slowdowns have stalled its progress, but China is still far ahead of the rest.

Can this be kept up? China is rich in natural resources, but its needs are so huge that it has to look overseas for oil, copper, or steel. As wages rise, so does the cost of goods, which makes export prices less competitive.

More than 3,000 workers produce garments at a factory in Longnan, central China. It is owned by Hong Kong–based Top Form International.

SHENZHEN SUPERLATIVES

Before 1979, Shenzhen, which is north of Hong Kong, was little more than a village. It was then developed by the government as a Special Economic Zone to attract foreign investment. That village has become a high-rise city and a part of a booming industrial region around the Zhujiang or Pearl River delta.

- Today, the zone is home to 15 million people.
- Shenzhen's industries include computer software, electronics, chemicals, and telecommunications.
- Its stock exchange is worth $1 trillion and makes approximately 600,000 deals a day.

China is the biggest coal producer in the world, but the work is poorly paid and can be dangerous.

THE POVERTY GAP

China's economic boom has created a class of rich managers, whose wages may equal those in the United States. China also has a wealthy city-based middle class. But a gulf has opened between the richest and poorest in society. For the unemployed, poor laborers, or peasant farmers, prosperity remains a dream. In 2011, about 13 percent of Chinese people lived below the poverty line, earning less than $363 per year. While it is a great improvement on the old days, it is still a harsh statistic.

TOWN AND COUNTRY

For thousands of years, most Chinese people were country dwellers, but that balance has changed. Half of the population now lives in towns and cities, and the number is growing year by year. China's peasants have always faced hardships, which include famine and floods. This shaped their values. They became a practical people who worked together to survive. Can these traditional values be transplanted to China's modern cities?

FIELDS AND VILLAGES

Many Chinese villages are made up of small cottages and built of clay brick or concrete with tiled roofs. Pigs, ducks, and chickens wander in the street. Corn cobs or chilli peppers are hung up to dry. Every scrap of land is cultivated — even in mountainous regions.

FARMING LIFE

In the north, fields of millet and wheat are tended while orchards growing apples or white Chinese pears. The misty hills of west central China are often bright yellow with oilseed rape. Lakes and rivers are fished with line and net. The farming year is an exhausting routine of plowing, planting, hoeing, reaping, and threshing. Southern landscapes include terraced hillsides for growing tea and paddy fields for wet rice cultivation with wallowing water buffalo.

Farmers work on the Dragon's Backbone rice terrace in Longsheng County, Guangxi. They can earn about $835 per year.

URBAN SHIFT

Since 1985, the gap in income between country and town has risen by 68 percent, so it is no wonder that so many rural workers leave for the cities. The 2010 census showed that 220 million Chinese people had worked away from their home for more than six months of the year.

East Nanjing Road in Shanghai is in of one of the world's busiest commercial centers.

LIFE IN THE CITY

Migrant laborers from the countryside are often treated poorly in Chinese cities. If they find work, most of their low pay is generally saved. Some end up living on the streets and struggling to survive.

Life is very different for wealthier city dwellers. They can afford to live in new high-rise apartments with four or more rooms. They might own comfortable sofas, a large-screen plasma television, and a washing machine. Buying fashionable clothes, traveling or eating out at restaurants are options. These would have been unheard of luxuries not so long ago.

FINANCIAL HUB

Beijing makes money. Modern hotels cater for the many tourists who come to explore the city and visit the Great Wall. The capital is a center for banking, insurance, and finance. The city is also the headquarters of many big Chinese and international companies. The chief business districts are along Financial Street and in the Guomao area. New electronic and computer technology is developed in the Zhongguancun district. Beijing has expensive shopping malls and car dealerships.

Most of the people on the city streets live on modest or low incomes. They have all sorts of jobs — waiters, road sweepers, laborers, bus drivers, cooks, or traders in the city's many markets. As elsewhere in China, the differences in income and working conditions is great. Many migrant workers from the countryside earn low pay and experience poor working conditions.

Beijing's industries include iron, steel, chemicals, oil refinery, electronics, telecommunications, and information technology. Most factories are on the outskirts of the city, but some of the dirtiest ones have been relocated in an effort to clean up the air. Vegetables are grown in the suburbs; crops such as wheat and maize are supplied from the surrounding countryside.

A baker sells buns in one of the few remaining hutong districts (see page 15) in Beijing. Street vendors are busy from breakfast until night. Steamed dumplings, egg pancakes, and buns stuffed with pork are popular snacks.

Most of Beijing's traditional hutongs have been demolished, but renovation offers work for bricklayers. A skilled builder can earn about $21.40 for a 10-hour day.

Cut flowers grown in the warm south go on sale at the end of January in Ditan Park, Beijing. A flower seller's busiest time is at Chinese New Year (the Spring Festival).

Beijing has about 67,000 taxis, which contribute to traffic congestion. Taxi drivers in Beijing often work a 14-hour day, which is over the legal limit. The company they work for can take a large share of their fares.

ON THE MOVE

A nation the size of China cannot function without good communications. Over the last 60 years, Chinese engineers have been pushing road and rail links through remote, difficult terrain. The 2006 rail link with Tibet reaches an altitude of 16,648 feet (5,072 m).

CHINA BY TRAIN

Most long journeys within China are taken by train, and railways also shift large amounts of freight. Stations are thronged with people, especially over Chinese New Year, when workers return home to their families and clutch bags full of gifts. Express trains offer several classes of travel. These include the crowded hard seats to the more comfortable soft sleepers.

CAR MAD

China has more than 2.3 million miles (3.8 million km) of roads, but the real transportation revolution is taking place on city streets. Towns used to swarm with bicycles as few people could afford to own cars. Now China manufactures one out of every four cars produced in the world. Taxi cabs, motorcycles, trucks, and buses add to city traffic jams and pollute the air.

National Highway 219 is one of the world's highest motorable roads. It crosses the harsh terrain from Xinjiang-Uyghur Autonomous Region into western Tibet.

The high-speed Shanghai Maglev (magnetic levitation) train uses magnets to glide above the track.

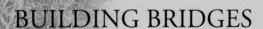

RIVER PORTS

China has more navigable waterways than any other country. Da Yunhe, the Grand Canal, has carried north-south traffic for more than 1,500 years. River steamers carry passengers from Chongqing down the Chang Jiang to Shanghai. Downstream dams are bypassed via locks with extreme drops. Traditional wooden boats carrying local produce can be seen alongside barges, bulk carriers, and car transporters.

INTERNATIONAL LINKS

Most overseas visitors arrive in China by plane. Beijing is the world's second busiest airport and offers internal flights all across China. Arrivals at Shanghai airport are whisked into the city by a futuristic Maglev train with a top speed of 268 miles per hour (431 kph). China's economy also depends on many big international seaports around eastern and southern coasts that are designed to handle ferries, oil tankers, and container ships.

BUILDING BRIDGES

When the Venetian merchant Marco Polo visited the Chinese city of Suzhou in 1276, he wrote that the city had 6,000 stone bridges! The Chinese are still building bridges today.

A complex of sea bridges across the Jiazhou bay, in Shandong province, opened in 2011. It links the city of Qingdao with neighboring districts and islands. It is also earthquake-proof. The total length of the bridges is a world record at 25.8 miles (41.6 km) and the project cost $9 billion.

An even bigger bridge and tunnel complex is planned to link Hong Kong, Zhuhai, and Macau in 2016 with a total length of 31 miles (50 km).

BIG ENGINEERING

The Chang Jiang is the world's third longest river with a length of 3,998 miles (6,418 km). It carries melting snow from the Qinghai-Tibet plateau eastward to the sea and powering its way through the beautiful Three Gorges region to the east of Chongqing. Its lower reaches are broad and slow, spilling across the great plain. The Chang Jiang basin drains 20 percent of all China and provides a home to one-third of the population. For nearly a century, Chinese politicians and engineers dreamed of taming the power of this mighty river by controlling its floods and generating power.

THREE GORGES DAM

Between 1994 and 2012 that dream was made a reality at the cost of about $42 billion. The river was dammed beneath the Three Gorges with a 1.2 miles (2 km) wall of concrete creating a reservoir 373 miles (600 km) long. By controlling the amount of water in the reservoir, the danger of severe flooding downstream was much reduced, and the conditions for shipping were improved. The Three Gorges Hydroelectric dam has 32 generators, each weighing about 6,600 tons (6,000 t), which can produce as much electricity as 11 nuclear power stations.

The Three Gorges Dam was the world's largest power station in terms of capacity in 2012.

Tamed at last, the waters of the Chang Jiang form a massive reservoir across the river valley.

CONCERNS

The dam project was a remarkable feat of engineering, but it has been widely criticized. Scenically, the rising water levels above the dam have reduced the impressive height of the Three Gorges. The huge mass of the reservoir is believed to have triggered landslides in the local area. The reservoir which also acts as a trap for industrial chemicals and city waste from upstream, which form a toxic lake.

THE HUMAN COST

The new reservoir drowned 13 cities, 140 towns, and 1,350 villages. Many historical and archaeological sites were flooded. More than 1.2 million people were forced from their homes. Many farmers and fishermen lost their work. Officials suppressed protest and compensation often was not paid.

A farmer watches on as the great dam is constructed. The displacement of people will increase the population of huge cities such as Chongqing.

AGAINST NATURE?

China's landscape has been shaped by human activity over the ages. The current population growth and spread of towns and factories are damaging the environment as never before. Such changes threaten the survival of many wild animals. These include the South China tiger, the Chinese alligator, and the giant panda.

AIR POLLUTION

China's factories use massive amounts of coal, oil, and gas. More than 7 percent of Chinese power stations also rely on carbon-based fuels, which makes China the world's worst air polluter. Smog blankets cities and damages health as well as the environment. The acid content of smoke that mixes with rain damages plants and buildings. Many scientists fear air pollution causes global climate change and are trying to agree to international cuts in carbon emissions. China feels that the developed countries, which became rich through industrializing back in the 1800s, should carry most of the cost and give newcomers time to catch up. China does agree to programs of carbon cutting, but many worry that these offer too little, too late.

Hunting and the loss of forests have endangered the South Chinese tiger. Fewer than 20 tigers may be surviving in the wild. None have actually been seen for more than 25 years.

SOIL, WIND, AND WATER

In many regions China's soil is often over farmed and treated with too much chemical fertilizer. As cities spread out into the countryside, forests are cut down. Roots can no longer hold the soil and keep it moist. It turns to dust and blows away with the wind. Deserts are increasing. As more and more water is needed, there severe shortages occur.

Since 1948, 20 percent of farmland has been lost to erosion or urban development. For a country that relies on home-grown crops to feed its growing population, this poses a serious danger.

A GREENER CHINA

China is taking steps to make things better. Some of the more polluting power plants have been shut down. A massive 22 percent of China's power is already generated by hydro-electric plans. Other renewable sources, such as sun and wind, provide another 2.3 percent. China is now a world leader in the production, trading, and installation of photovoltaic technology, which generates power from solar radiation. In recent years, ordinary people across the country have become more aware of the environment. Many protest in public against factory pollution and take part in tree-planting programs.

China is investing in tree planting. These are designed to halt the spread of the Gobi Desert into northern China.

CHINESE SOCIETY
SEEKING JUSTICE

Prisoners are seated on rows of benches for a public address at Foshan Labor Camp in Guandong province.

China has had a low crime rate for many years. But signs of violent crimes are on the increase. One reason may be the growing gap between rich and poor.

THE LAW

Many Chinese laws are similar to those in other countries, but the courts are not independent from government. The National People's Congress appoints judges to the Supreme Court. The interests of the state are seen as more important than individual rights. However, reforms were passed in 1996 and 2012, to bring in jurors and give greater rights to defendants.

PUNISHMENT

Court sentences are harsh. In 2008, China had 350 labor camps where offenders could spend up to four years without a trial. In 2012, after growing public opposition, the government announced that this policy was being reconsidered. The number of offenses carrying the death penalty was also to be reviewed. China executed more prisoners than any other nation in 2013. The exact number is unknown, but it may have been as many as 4,000.

HUMAN RIGHTS

International campaigners criticize China's record on human rights. They point to the lack of free speech and basic political or religious freedoms (refer to page 37). They criticize the system of justice and capital punishment, dissidents may be shut away in psychiatric institutions. China's hardline treatment of campaigners for Tibetan independence has met with protests around the world.

Some leading Chinese figures have become famous for criticizing government policies. The number of ordinary Chinese people who dare to protest about human rights is small, but their number is growing.

The popular artist and political activist Ai Weiwei has become a thorn in the flesh of the Chinese government.

AN ARTIST PROTESTS

Ai Weiwei (born 1957) is a Chinese artist and architect. He is best known as the artistic consultant for the National Stadium for the 2008 Beijing Olympics (refer to page 15).

However, Ai has become even better known as a critic of the Chinese record on human rights.

- He criticized the Olympic Games organizers.

- He blamed poor building standards for deaths in the 2008 Sichuan earthquake.

- He protested against air pollution in China's cities and photographed himself in a gas mask.

- He mocked the Chinese government with photographs and performance art.

Over the years, the Chinese authorities have responded by closing down Ai Weiwei's studio, charging him with not paying taxes, putting him in prison, and refusing him foreign travel permits.

HEALTH AND LEARNING

When the first American fast-food chain opened in China in 1990, a customer was asked what he thought of the food. He looked puzzled and said, "Is it supposed to taste like that?" Today, Western fast foods are so popular in the cities that they are causing a worrying rise in obesity. Another habit has caused a health problem for many years. China is the world's biggest producer of tobacco. Despite campaigns, many Chinese remain smokers.

HEALTHCARE

Smoking and air pollution are two reasons why cancer, heart disease, and breathing problems are common diseases in China. However, most Chinese women can expect to live to more than 77 and men to about 73 years. China spends more than 4 percent of its GDP on health care — about half the proportion spent in Britain or Japan. City hospitals are better equipped than those in the country, but most villages have medical clinics. China has moved away from the communist ideal of free health care for all. This has led to hardship for poorer people as welfare allowances are cut. A health insurance system is now in place, and private medical care is available for those who can afford it. In 2012, the Chinese government proposed a huge increase in funding to meet the health needs of all.

American fast food is on sale in Xianyang. Increased prosperity is rapidly changing people's diet in China's cities.

HERBS AND ACUPUNCTURE

In China, bundles of herbs and other traditional medications are often on sale. Acupuncture, a treatment with fine needles, is another popular way of dealing with medical problems.

LEARNING

Education has a very ancient history in China. The tradition is to learn by rote and then be tested. Less emphasis is given on individualism or challenging questions. Children have to spend at least nine years at school. Primary education lasts from the age of 6 or 7 until 12. Secondary schools are attended between 12 and 18. At one time, China had no private schools. In another departure from communist principles for the government, wealthier families now use private schools. Recent years have seen a great increase in enrollment at the country's 2,000 universities and colleges, which have about six million student places. Rising fees have hit poorer students, despite loan plans. Wealthier students may study at private colleges or overseas.

LITERACY LEAP

While children in Europe or the United States may struggle with an alphabet of 26 letters, Chinese school children learn at least 3,000–4,000 characters! These symbols represent words or sounds. Before 1949, 80 percent of the population could not read or write. Today 92 percent of people over the age of 15 are literate.

Jars of traditional Chinese medicines. Some of these treatments have been used in China for more than 2,000 years.

MEDIA MESSAGES

The Chinese have been writing for more than 3,000 years. Their literature includes poetry and novels. Paper was invented 2,000 years ago in China. What may be the oldest book in the world to have survived, the Diamond Sutra, was printed in China in 868. Approximately 600 years ago, China produced Yongle Dadian—the encyclopedia of its day. Written by 2,000 scholars on scrolls, it makes 11,095 volumes!

Newspaper and magazine sales in China are increasing, while they are falling in Europe and North America.

MAINSTREAM MEDIA

Today, words still spin off China's printing presses. More than 96 million national and regional newspapers are sold every day. As many as 6.44 billion books are printed each year. Other communications media also are booming. Television and radio offer more than 2,000 channels or stations at the national, provincial, or city level. All are owned or approved by the Communist Party or the state. Journalists who step out of line risk imprisonment (see opposite).

Customers log on at an Internet cafe in Chengdu, Sichuan province. The meteoric rise of the Internet is being monitored closely by the government.

POLICING THE PRESS

In January 2013, approximately 100 journalists working on the Guangdong newspaper, *Southern Weekend,* went on strike. In most countries, this would not be unusual, but in China this news was sensational.

- **Why did the journalists stop work?** The propaganda chief for Guangdong province had axed an article in the newspaper that called for human rights to be protected. He replaced it with an article praising the Chinese Communist Party. The journalists claimed he had misrepresented them on the newspaper's microblog and stated that more than 1,000 articles in the paper had been censored in the previous year.

- **What did the public think?** A crowd of sympathizers soon gathered outside the newspaper offices. Students, lawyers, and other journalists all expressed their support.

- **Were the strikers punished?** It was agreed that no action would be taken against them, so they returned to work. However, Internet access to sites reporting this story was blocked.

CHINA ONLINE

It is much easier for governments to control and regulate traditional publishing and broadcasting than the new electronic media. China has an incredible 986 million cell phones. It has more Internet users than any other nation — about 389 million. As there is great enthusiasm for popular fiction, many writers self-publish online. A huge number of Internet users log into a microblogging site called Sina Weibo. It is similar to Twitter and gets about 100 million messages posted every day. Sina Weibo is a symbol of how much China has changed and how it is speeding up that change.

THE GREAT FIREWALL OF CHINA

It is hard for any one nation to control or censor the media in the global age of the Internet. China has shut down websites and blocked access to foreign media sites including Facebook and Twitter. This policy has been called "the Great Firewall of China". Like the Great Wall, China is unlikely to be able to hold back outside influences forever.

ARTS AND ARENAS

The way in which people express and enjoy themselves can reveal a great deal. China has a rich culture that has evolved over thousands of years. Its common themes include a love of harmony, balance, and simple beauty, all of which are deeply rooted in ancient spiritual beliefs.

ART AND CRAFT

The first Chinese poetry was closely linked with music. Writing merged with the visual arts in calligraphy — the beautiful painting of Chinese characters or symbols. Chinese craft skills also produced fine porcelain pottery and luxurious silk textiles.

Chinese music was very different from European music. It could be graceful, or dramatic with crashing gongs, bells, and drums. Performance arts included acrobatics, juggling, and popular Chinese operas. Heroes and villains with painted faces or masks and elaborate costumes played out dramatic tales.

CULTURE AND CHANGE

In the 1950s and 1960s, Western styles of art and music were frowned upon, but Chinese arts such as calligraphy were encouraged. However, all the arts were expected to serve Communist ideals. Traditional Chinese operas were updated as revolutionary propaganda.

Today, artists in China have greater freedom. Chinese art and the work of filmmakers have become very popular internationally. Films such as the action comedy *Let the Bullets Fly*, directed by Jiang Wen in 2010, have been hugely popular with the Chinese public. Other filmmakers are taking on social issues such as migration into the cities. However, artists making political statements still need to be very careful.

Drama and color... traditional opera, called "Monkey King: Flaming Mountain," is staged by the Sichuan Opera Theatre company.

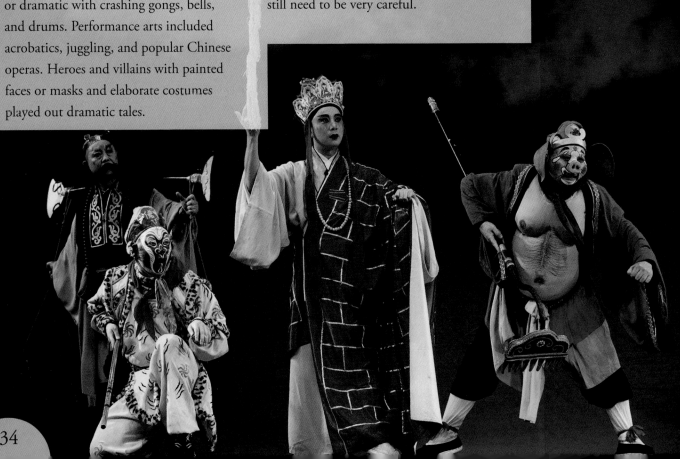

LEISURE

Parks are often the best place to see how people in China spend their leisure time. They may gather to make music, play cards, or have a game of Chinese chess. People may be practicing the slow moves of taijiquan (*tai chi*), which is a traditional martial art that is also a good way to relax and keep fit.

SPORTS

Table tennis is a popular sport in China and has produced many internationally successful players. The Beijing Olympics of 2008 put Chinese sports under the international spotlight and gave a big boost to badminton, basketball, volleyball, and swimming. At the highest level, city-based soccer clubs compete in a Chinese Super League. Chinese soccer fans often follow the European game, and major Chinese players have signed up to play for British and German teams.

Synchronized diving champions Chen Ruolin and Wang Xin celebrate winning gold at the 2008 Beijing Olympics.

Taijiquan is a great way to start the day. It also helps to relieve the stress of city life.

35

BELIEFS AND FESTIVALS

Emei Shan, in Sichuan province, is one of China's holy mountains. Walking up trails through forests, you come across beautiful, old Buddhist temples. Incense sticks are placed before statues. Emei Shan may seem to be a world away from the materialistic life of the big cities, but its traditional beliefs have always shaped Chinese society.

The Golden Summit at the top of Mount Emei is regarded as one of the four sacred Buddhist mountains in China.

THREE TRADITIONS

Three philosophies took root in China in ancient times — Daoism, Confucianism, and Buddhism. They existed alongside each other until they gradually intertwined and became seen as paths to the same truth. They developed rituals and religious ceremonies. Sometimes these were mixed with much older beliefs in spirits and magic. The teachings of Lao Zi, Kong Fuzi (Confucius), and Gautama Buddha (the founder of Buddhism) that the Chinese developed an understanding of the natural way of the world, respect for ancestors, ideals of compassion, and duties to family and nation. Buddhism took many forms in China with a separate branch of the faith developing in Tibet, Mongolia, and northeast China.

RELIGION AND POLITICS

In 1949, the new Communist government was officially atheist. It claimed that religion held back social progress. During the Cultural Revolution (the period of political unrest in the 1960s), activists tried to ban all worship and destroy religious buildings. Many of these buildings now have been restored. Today, religious worship is permitted and nearly one-third of China's population may be religious believers. Five main Chinese-based religious organizations (Buddhist, Daoist, Protestant, Catholic, and Muslim) are officially recognized. Unregistered sects harassed by the authorities, may choose to worship in secret.

The Chinese New Year is the biggest festival of the year and is celebrated around the world.

ISLAM AND CHRISTIANITY

Islam arrived in China in the 7th century BC. Today, the Hui is still a large Chinese Muslim community. Their Grand Mosque is in the historic city of Xian, which is in the northwest province of Shaanxi. Islam is also followed by Uyghurs and Tajiks living in China's far west. Christianity arrived at around the same time as Islam, and it was mostly spread by Western missionaries in the 1800s and 1900s.

FIRECRACKERS AND DRAGONS

Most Chinese people today are not religious. However, they are often superstitious about lucky numbers or good fortune. They enjoy seasonal and regional festivals. The Chinese New Year — known to the Chinese as the Spring Festival — is celebrated with firecrackers, drums, cymbals, and dragon and lion dancers.

FOCUS ON BEIJING: RELAX!

Even in times of hardship, the Chinese people always manage to find ways to enjoy themselves through music, performance, art, or simple fun. These days, Beijing offers more entertainment possibilities than ever before.

A symbol of change can be seen in Dashanzi, which is in Beijing's Chaoyang district. A former military factory space has been taken over as a lively center of international artistic creativity known as the 798 Art Zone.

Beijing's theaters offer traditional, spectacular Beijing operas, as well as circus skills or martial arts displays. At the Beijing Dance Academy, students learn classical ballet.

China is famous for its tasty cuisine. Most of its regional styles of food can be tried in Beijing. Its own claim to fame is crispy roasted duck. Popular restaurants offer a huge choice of dishes, which seem to make use of every possible part of an animal or plant. Nothing goes to waste in a Chinese kitchen!

In winter families might go skating in Beihai Park. In many spring take a boat out on the lake at Yiheyuan (the New Summer Palace). An old man might sit on a bench in the summer sunshine with his memories — and his caged birds.

Visitors become part of the exhibits at the 798 Art Zone, which is a center of experimental painting and sculpture.

When the lake freezes over in Beihai Park, it's time to wrap up warm and go skating. In January, daytime temperatures may be just above freezing point, dropping to about 16°F (-9°C) overnight.

A group of friends meets up for an open air lunch on a sunny day in Beijing.

The er hu is a traditional two-stringed fiddle and is played with a bow. Heard in parks and on the streets, it is often played by blind entertainers.

Keeping caged birds is a traditional hobby in China. Older men often take their pets to the park for sunshine and fresh air.

39

CHAPTER 4

CHINA & THE WORLD
CHINA INTERNATIONAL

Chinese workers have settled in other parts of the world for hundreds of years. From London to San Francisco and from Singapore to Sydney, there are long established Chinese communities have established markets, businesses, and cultural centers. Chinese languages are spoken as a first language by approximately 1.2 billion people worldwide. Now that China has opened up to the outside world, its international role is more important than ever.

Dating back to 1848, Chinatown in San Francisco is home to the oldest Chinese community in the United States.

TRADE AND RESOURCES

Most often, new links are based upon business, trade, and investment. If trade does not flow both ways equally, there can be problems. For example, the United States buys far more Chinese goods than China buys American goods. In 2012, this trade gap reached a record high. Still, business relationships can have other advantages that lead to cooperation in education, sciences, the arts, or sports.

China's search for resources is on a massive scale. It has led China to buy up mines or huge areas of overseas farmland from Africa to South America. Such business deals are often welcomed, especially if they bring another country much needed road building and development. At other times they can lead to tensions with local communities and workers (see box on page 41).

Local workers sort ore under Chinese supervision at a depot in the Katanga region of the Democratic Republic of Congo.

CHINESE IN AFRICA

Chinese ships have visited Africa for centuries. Today, natural resources, such as metal and oil, are the main attraction. The Chinese have invested more than $1 billion in Zambia's copper mines. For example, as many as 10,000 Chinese people live and work in Zambia. Some work as builders and market traders; others run mines or textile factories.

In much of Africa, Chinese investment has been welcomed. However, Zambia has experienced violent wage disputes at Chinese-run mines. Widespread complaints note that Chinese incomers are taking jobs away from local people.

MAPS AND BORDERS

Most countries have disputes about their borders from time to time. China shares its frontiers with no fewer than 14 other nations. In the past China has had border disputes with India, Russia, and Vietnam, but these have been settled.

Rivalry for offshore oil reserves cause new disputes. Southeast Asian nations argue about maritime boundaries and the ownership of islands in the South China Sea. Although Japan and China are big trading partners, historical tensions are rooted in the Japanese invasions from 1931 to 1945.

"TAIWAN, PROVINCE OF CHINA"

Taiwan is another political flashpoint. The Nationalist Chinese set up a government on this island in 1949 when the Communists came to power in Beijing. Taiwan claimed to represent the whole of China and was strongly supported by the United States. In turn, the People's Republic claimed Taiwan as one of its provinces. From time to time, military exercises along the Taiwan Strait raise international tension.

LOOKING TO THE FUTURE

Coming down to Earth. Liu Yang waves as she emerges from the reentry capsule after her space flight.

On June 16, 2012, Liu Yang became the first Chinese woman in space. Her spacecraft, *Shenzhou 9*, was launched by rocket from the Gobi Desert. It docked with the *Tiangong 1* space station two days later. Liu Yang was born in 1978 — two years after the death of Mao Zedong. Her achievement showed just how far China has advanced its technology.

BIG QUESTIONS

The Chinese philosopher Lao Zi wrote: "The flame that burns twice as bright burns half as long." China's future could be very bright, but nothing is certain. Can China find the resources it needs? Can it pay higher wages and still compete internationally? Can it develop further without ruining the environment and its heritage? If China makes political reforms, will it still be able to direct its economy as effectively? China spends large amounts of money on the military. Can it live in peace with its neighbors? Can this country manage a society that is divided by wealth, or can it build a more equal and just society that respects human rights?

WAYS FORWARD

These questions apply not only to China but to nations around the world. Sustainability, the environment, economics, growth, and human rights are issues for us all. If there is a difference, it is the sheer size and the scale of the problems for the world's largest population. As Liu Yang looked back at Earth, the planet looked small in the vastness of space. That image reminds us that we must work together for a better future. What kind of nation China will become is unknown. However, if we look at 2,000 years of history three themes stand out from China's past: resilience, inventiveness, and continuity.

Fishing with tame cormorants on the River Li. As China moves forward, it must value and take strength from its ancient traditions.

43

GLOSSARY

acupuncture a method of treating pain or illness using fine needles

autonomous region a part of China that has a regional government with rights to pass some of its own laws

basin an area of land drained by a river and its tributaries

calligraphy handwriting as a form of art

capital (1) the chief city in a nation or region, often the center of government (2) wealth in the form of money or property and is used for business or finance

capitalism an economic system based on private ownership and the accumulation of private wealth

census an official count of the population

character a symbol that represents a sound or word in the Chinese language

climate change a change in the climate experienced in a region or in the world as a whole

colony a country or territory governed or settled by another nation

communications media any method of communicating, such as broadcasting, books, newspapers, movies, television, or the Internet

communism a social and economic system based on common ownership or state control in the interest of working people

corruption dishonest behavior, such as accepting bribes

Cultural Revolution an attempt to rally radical support for Mao Zedong in the period 1966–68 that resulted in social chaos, violence, and destruction

defendant the accused person during a trial

delta an area where silt has built up at a river mouth, and creates a number of separate waterways

dissident someone who disagrees with the government or society

emission the release of gases into the atmosphere, such as exhaust fumes from traffic

empire lands that have been brought together under the rule of a single government or emperor

erosion the wearing down of a landscape by wind, water, frost, or heat

ethnic group part of a population sharing the same way of life, customs, beliefs, ancestry, or language

faction a small group within a political party or government

firewall in computing, hardware or software that keeps a network secure or isolated

human rights the basic needs required for people to be treated with justice and equality

hydroelectric power generated from the movement of water

innovation bringing in new ideas or technologies

investment putting money into an enterprise in order to make more money

labor camp a camp where prisoners are forced to carry out hard work, such as breaking stones

literate able to read and write

lock a section of a river or canal with a barrier, that allows boats to be lowered or raised from one level to another

Maglev magnets raise the train from the rails, reducing friction

migrant laborer someone who moves from one part of the country to another in search of work

missionary a religious person sent abroad to spread the faith

municipality in China, a division of regional government based upon a large city and the surrounding countryside

nationalist 1) someone campaigning for their land to become independent or free of foreign control 2) people promoting the interest of their own nation above all others

nationalize to place a private company or service under state ownership

natural resource any naturally occurring material that can be used in manufacturing or supply, such as coal, iron, water, or timber

navigable rivers, lakes, or seas able to be navigated by a ship

obesity being overweight

paddy field an area of flooded land used for growing rice

philosophy the study of knowledge, existence, truth, and wisdom

photovoltaic converting rays from the sun into electricity

plateau an expanse of flat land set at a high altitude

pollute to poison the land, water, or air with chemical or other waste matter

poverty line the lowest level of income required to meet basic needs

propaganda information or misinformation designed to promote a political party or a government, or used to denigrate opponents

prosecution lawyers or other legal officials who make the case against defendants in courts of law

province in China, a region of administration and local government

reach an open stretch of a winding river course

renewable not depending on resources that will run out; wind, sun, and waves are all renewable energy sources

republic a country ruled by the people rather than by a king, queen, or emperor

reservoir an area or containment used to store a large mass of water

rote memorize words, facts, or figures

shareholder someone who buys shares in a company to make money from the company's profits

social media online sites that encourage the exchange of information and ideas between individuals and groups

Special Administrative Regions parts of China which have their own economic and political system, namely the former colonies of Macau (Portugal) and Hong Kong (Britain)

Special Economic Zone a region of China that encourages foreign investment and the development of new industries

steppes wide open areas of natural grassland

stock exchange a financial center for the buying and selling of shares

subtropical bordering Earth's tropical regions

Supreme Court in many countries, the name given to the highest court of law

toxic poisonous

trade gap the difference between the value of imports and exports

typhoon a tropical storm, the east Asian name for a hurricane

visual arts arts based on appearance, such as painting, photography, or sculpture

welfare economic or other support given to an individual or family by the government

FURTHER INFORMATION

BOOKS

Eyewitness: Ancient China, Arthur Cotterell (Dorling Kindersley, 2005)

Atlas of China, (National Geographic, 2009)

Countries in Our World: China, Oliver James (Smart Apple Media, 2011)

Modern China: A Very Short Introduction, Rana Mitter (OUP Oxford 2008)

WEBSITES

www.guardian.co.uk/world/interactive/2012/mar/23/china-decade-change-interactive-timeline
A very useful interactive timeline showing events from recent Chinese politics, economics, development, and other areas of interest.

www.chinatoday.com
A portal with links to Chinese and international media and a very wide range of topics.

www.travel.nationalgeographic.com/travel/countries/china-guide
Pictures and articles on ancient and modern China, Chinese culture, and travel.

Every effort has been made by the publishers to ensure that the websites in this book are suitable for children and that they contain no inappropriate or offensive material. However, because of the nature of the Internet, it is impossible to guarantee that the contents of these sites will not be altered. We strongly advise that Internet access is supervised by a responsible adult.

INDEX